Where Do People Work?

by Helen Gregory

Consultant:
Adria F. Klein, Ph.D.
California State University, San Bernardino

capstone classroom
Heinemann Raintree • Red Brick Learning
division of Capstone

People work in our town.

Many people work.

People work in schools.

Teachers work in the classroom.

Principals work in the school office.

Clerks work in stores.

Police officers work in police cars.

Firefighters work in firetrucks.

Reporters work in offices.

Doctors work in hospitals.

Dentists work in offices.

Scientists work in labs.

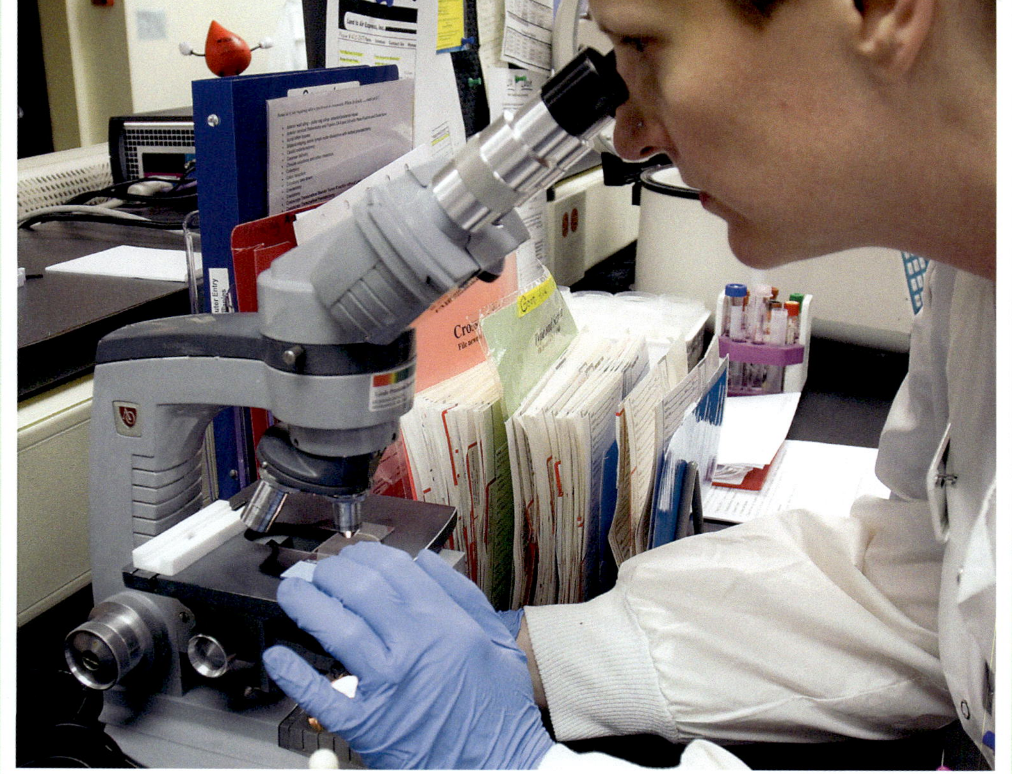

Construction workers work in big machines.

Gardeners work outside.

People work at home, too.